ISBN 979-8-218-32413-1

Author: Kholofelo Mothibi
Inspired by: Moloko Rakabe
Illustration Concept: Palesa Rakabe
Illustrated by: Natali Kholodniak

For permissions requests, contact: Kholofelo.mothibi@icloud.com

Author's Note

"Mo and Sibi's Journey: Discovering Fairness and Equality" has been a labor of love, inspired by my nephews, Linda Mabece, Moloko, and Mohau Rakabe. Their endless curiosity and boundless energy sparked the idea for this book, setting me on a year-long journey to bring this story to life.

Their questions about the world, eagerness to learn, and innate sense of justice reminded me how important it is to teach young minds about history and empathy. This book aims to nurture that same curiosity in other children, encouraging them to explore, ask questions, and understand the significance of kindness and equality.

Writing this book has been incredibly rewarding. I hope that "Mo and Sibi" will inspire many young readers to be curious, compassionate, and courageous in their everyday lives. Thank you to my nephews for being the bright light that guided me on this incredible journey.

This book is dedicated to my nieces and nephews. May their curiosity inspire positive change in the world

Mo and Sibi's Journey:

DISCOVERING FAIRNESS AND EQUALITY

By Kholofelo Mothibi

illustrated by Natali Kholodniak

inspired by Moloko Rakabe

"Hello! I'm Moloko, but you can call me Mo. This is my dog, Sibi – he's my best buddy. We love playing and listening to stories from my grandma. Isn't that right, Sibi?"

"Woof, woof!"

"Today we're going on an adventure to share a special story from the past! It's a story about how people weren't always treated the same, and how some very brave people stood up for what was right. They wanted to make the world a fair place for everyone."

"Sibi, are you ready?"

"Woof, woof!"

"Let's begin our adventure,"

"Lunchtime is my favorite part of the day,"

"My friends, Star, Leo, and I always have so much fun playing on the playground."

Mo looked over and saw something troubling.

"Hey, did you see what those older kids did?"

"Yeah,"

Leo replied

"They didn't let Dineo play on the swings."

Mo frowned.

"That's not fair. Everyone should be able to play on the playground."

Just then, the school bell rang, signaling the end of lunchtime. Mo and his friends knew it was time to go back to class, but Mo couldn't stop thinking about how sad Dineo must have felt.

After school, Mo rushed home and found his grandma in the kitchen.

"Grandma, today at school, some older kids wouldn't let Dineo play on the swings,"

Mo said, feeling upset.

"That must have been really hard for Dineo. It's not always easy to know what to do, Mo. But doing the right thing is always important."

Mo nodded thoughtfully, then went outside to play with Sibi while Grandma made dinner.

While playing outside, **Sibi** noticed something shiny poking out from under a loose stone. "Sibi dug under and around the stone and pulled out an old key."

Sibi ran excitedly towards Mo,

"Woof, woof!"

he barked, holding the key tightly in his mouth.

"What did you find, Sibi? I've never seen a key like this before. I wonder what it opens."

Come on, Sibi, let's go find out"
Mo said, heading back to the house

Mo and Sibi began their search, exploring every corner of the house—the garage with its dusty trunks, and every room in Grandma's house—but the key didn't fit any of the locks.

"Mo! Sibi! What are you up to?"

Grandma called out with a smile.

"Sorry for the mess, Grandma! We found a mysterious key,"

Mo explained.

Grandma looked at the key thoughtfully.

"Let me see that. Where did you find this old key?"

she asked, smiling and hugging Mo.

"In the garden,"

Mo replied.

Grandma's eyes twinkled.

**"This is for my special album.
Come, let's go get it."**

Grandma pulled out an old, dusty album from a shelf. As she opened it, dust flew everywhere, making them all sneeze.

"Achoo!"
Mo sneezed.

"Achoo!"
Sibi sneezed, shaking his head.

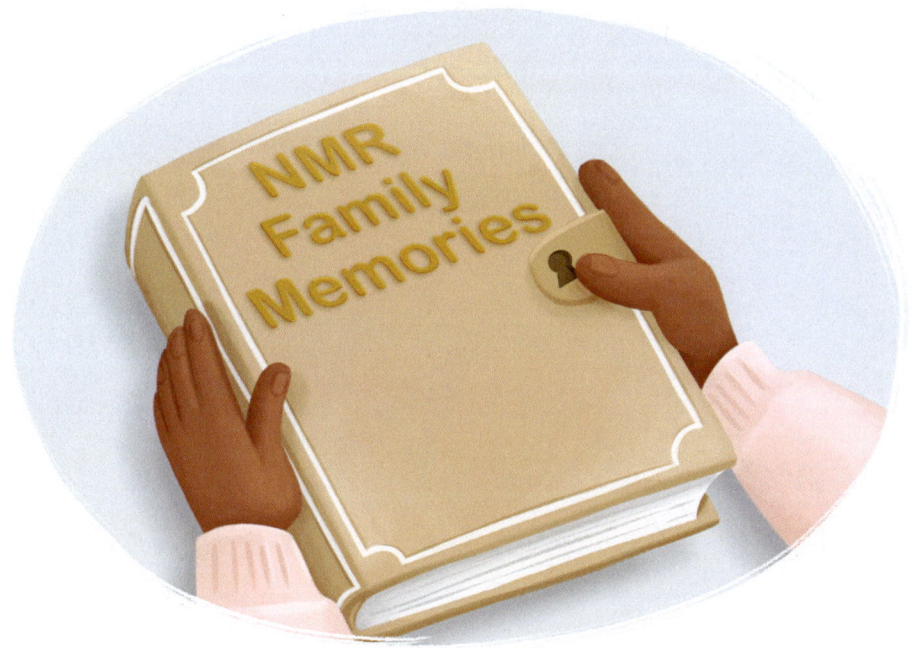

Grandma smiled as she wiped down the album.

**"This album holds many memories.
Let me open it up and show you some
of the photos."**

Mo looked at the black-and-white photos curiously.

"Why do the photos have no color?"

he asked.

"They were taken a long time ago,"

Grandma explained with a laugh.

Mo pointed at a photo.

"Who is that in the first photo?"
he asked.

"That's me when
I was about your age,"
Grandma replied.

"Why do you look
sad, Grandma?"
Mo asked.

"I lived in a time when things were tough, and smiles were hard to find,"

Grandma said softly.

"Why was it tough?"

Mo asked, puzzled.

"There was a time when people were not treated the same,"

Grandma explained.

Mo looked puzzled.
"What do you mean, Grandma?"
he asked.

Grandma sighed.

"Not everyone was allowed to play together, go to the same schools, or even live in the same neighborhoods because of a law called apartheid,"
she explained.

"What is apartheid?"
Mo asked.

"Apartheid meant that the government could treat people differently based on the color of their skin. People did not have equal rights,"
Grandma said.

"What are equal rights?"
Mo asked.

"Equal rights mean treating all people the same, no matter who they are or what they look like,"
Grandma explained.

Historical Note:

Apartheid was a system in South Africa that kept people apart based on their skin color. It lasted for 46 years, from 1948 to 1994. Many brave people worked hard to end apartheid so everyone could be treated equally.

"Imagine if you couldn't sit next to your friend in class or play with them at the park because a rule said you couldn't. That would feel very unfair, wouldn't it?"

Grandma asked.

"Yes!"

Mo exclaimed.

"It was a sad time, but people came together to make a change,"

Grandma continued.

"What kind of change?"

Mo asked.

"Where everyone is treated the same, no matter who they are or what they look like,"

Grandma explained.

Mo pointed to another photo.
"Grandma, is that you in this photo?"
he asked.

"Yes, this was a march led by activists who stood up against apartheid,"
Grandma explained.

"What are activists?"
Mo asked.

FREEDOM, EQUALITY NO APARTHEID!!!!

"Activists are people who work to make change. They help everyone by standing up for what's right,"
Grandma said.

"Like Nelson Mandela!"
Mo exclaimed.

"Yes, like Nelson Mandela! He believed in equality, and because of his work and the work of many others, the laws of apartheid were changed,"

Grandma said.

"He was like a superhero!"

Mo said.

"He was, Mo. And just like superheroes, he had a lot of friends who helped him. They worked together to make the world a better place,"

Grandma said.

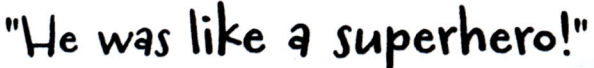

Interactive Prompt:
Who is your favorite superhero? Why?

Historical Note:
In 1994, Nelson Mandela became the first Black president of South Africa. This was the first time that everyone, no matter their skin color, could vote. Today, April 27 is celebrated as Freedom Day to remember when South Africa began a new chapter of fairness and equality for all.

"Who were some of his friends, Grandma?"
Mo asked.

"There were heroes like Desmond Tutu, who spoke out for peace and fairness; Albertina Sisulu, who stood up for women's rights; Winnie Madikizela-Mandela, who helped bring people together to stand up for freedom; and Oliver Tambo, who told the world about the unfair laws and helped unite people to change them. Together with many others, their voices grew strong like a big, mighty tree,"

Grandma explained.

"That's amazing, Grandma, like superheroes working together!"

Mo said.

"Yes, from all over South Africa and the world, people came together. They showed that by working together and standing up for what is right, we can make the world a better place."

Grandma said.

Historical Note:
Nelson Mandela, Desmond Tutu, Albertina Sisulu, Winnie Madikizela-Mandela, and Oliver Tambo were just a few of the many brave leaders who stood up against the unfair apartheid laws in South Africa. Together with countless other heroes and activists, their courage helped change the country for the better.

"These activists were young and old, and came from all different backgrounds,"

Grandma explained.

"Like a rainbow in the sky, Grandma!"

Mo said.

"Yes, that's a great example, Mo. They taught us that anyone can stand up for what is right and make a difference,"

Grandma said.

"Grandma, can Sibi and I make a difference like the activists?"

Mo asked.

"Yes, Mo! Everyone can help make things better,"

Grandma said.

Historical Note:

After apartheid ended, South Africa became known as the "Rainbow Nation." This was to celebrate the country's many different cultures and people coming together as one. It shows that just like a rainbow has many colors, South Africa is beautiful because of its diversity.

"Thanks to the courage of many people and activists who believed in fairness, things started to change for the better,"
Grandma said.

"Now we can all play, laugh, and live together,"
Mo said.

"Fairness and equality are like seeds that have grown into a beautiful garden where every plant is unique but equal,"
Grandma said.

"Like your garden, Grandma!"
Mo said with a smile.

Interactive Prompt:
What are some ways you can show kindness to others?

"The activists made a BIG difference. They remind us that no matter how young we are, we can be brave and change the world,"

Mo said.

"Woof, woof!"
Sibi barked proudly.

Mo laughed.
"You too,
Sibi."

"When we speak up for fairness and equality, our voice is powerful!" Grandma said.

"What can we do to remember the activists?" Mo asked.

"Keep telling their stories," Grandma replied.

The next day at school, Mo gathered his friends during lunchtime. They sat in a circle, eager to share their thoughts.

"You know, those older kids not letting Dineo play on the swings wasn't right,"

Mo said.

"Yeah, it wasn't right at all,"

Star agreed.

"My grandma told me about people called activists. They stood up for what was right, even when it was hard,"

Mo explained.

"Really? What did they do?"

Leo asked.

"They worked to make sure everyone was treated equally and fairly,"

Mo replied.

"Like superheroes?"

Star asked

"Exactly!"

Mo said with a smile.

"Let's tell the teachers so they can help make sure everyone gets a turn,"

Mo said enthusiastically.

Interactive Prompt: How can you be a superhero in your own way?

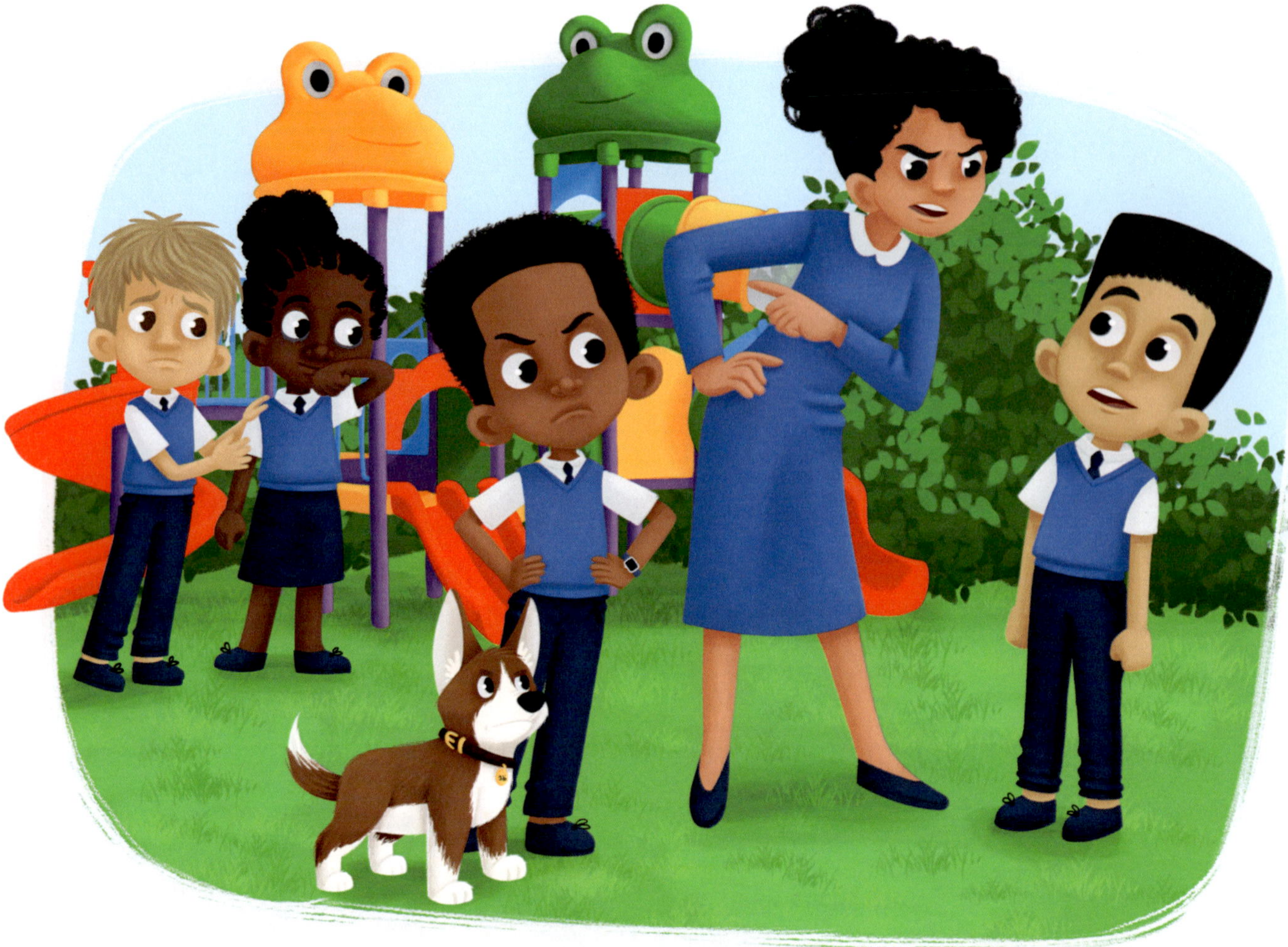

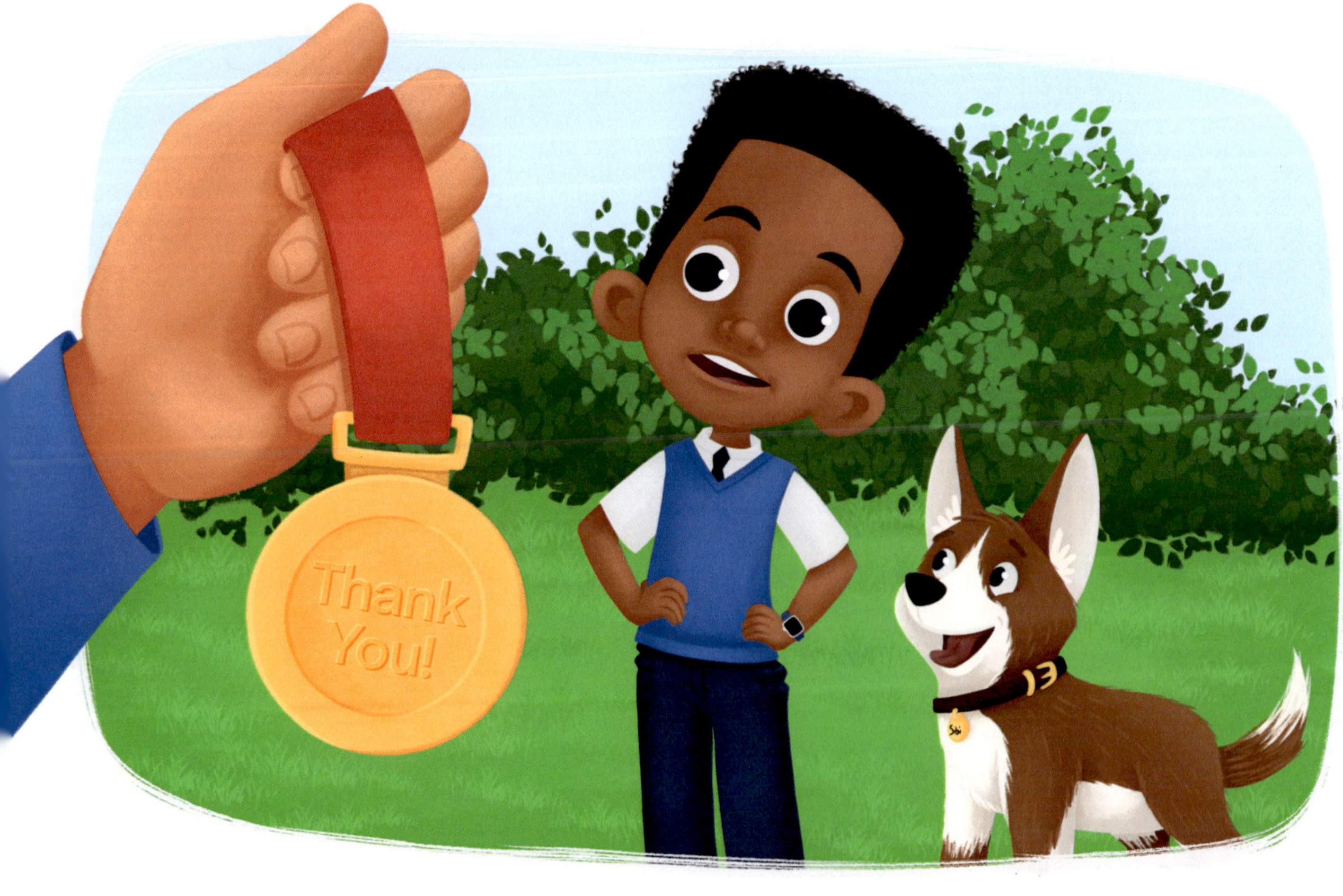
Thank You!

"Today, I remembered what you taught me, Grandma. When I saw someone being treated unfairly at school, I stood up for them, just like the activists did,"

Mo said proudly.

"I am so proud of you, Mo. You did the right thing,"

Grandma replied.

"Thank you, Grandma, for teaching us about courage and kindness. We've learned so much from you,"

Mo said.

"Always remember, Mo, it's important to stand up for what's right, and small actions can make a difference,"

Grandma said.

"Yes, they do, Grandma,"

Mo agreed.

"Woof!"
Sibi barked happily.

Notes for Parents, Teachers, and Caregivers:

The 1913 Native Land Act:

The 1913 Native Land Act was one of the first major segregation laws passed in South Africa. It became law on 19 June 1913, limiting native black land ownership to 7%, which was later increased to 13% through the 1936 Native Trust and Land Act of South Africa. The Act restricted black people from buying or occupying land. It opened the door for white ownership of 87% of land. This law forced many black families off their land and into overcrowded and impoverished areas. Once the law was passed, the apartheid government began the mass relocation of black people to poor homelands and poorly planned townships.

What is Apartheid?

Apartheid was a system of laws in South Africa that separated people based on their skin color. These laws were created to keep different racial groups apart and treated some people unfairly.

When Did Apartheid Start and End?

Apartheid started in 1948 and was officially dismantled by 1994. During this period, the South African government imposed strict policies that segregated people by race and limited their rights and freedoms. In 1992, a referendum showed strong support for ending apartheid, leading to the first democratic elections in 1994.

Race Classifications:

Under apartheid, people in South Africa were classified into different racial groups: Black, White, Coloured (Mixed race), and Indian. The racial classifications governed many aspects of daily life and used to enforce segregation and discriminatory policies. These laws dictated where individuals could reside, their employment opportunities, educational facilities they could attend, and even whom they could marry. The policies enforced strict racial segregation and created significant inequalities, deeply impacting the lives of non-white South Africans.

The First Democratic Election:

The first democratic election where everyone in South Africa was eligible to vote, regardless of race, was held in 1994. Nelson Mandela was elected the first black president in post-apartheid South Africa.

Marches are when a group of people walk together to show that they care deeply about something. In history, many people have marched to stand up for fairness and to make their voices heard. In South Africa, during the time of apartheid, people marched to protest unfair laws that treated people differently because of their skin color. These marches helped show the world that people wanted change.

Post-Apartheid:

South Africa has grown into an inclusive society where people of all colors live together, learn from each other, and share in the country's journey forward. Schools, parks, and neighborhoods now welcome everyone, celebrating the beauty of diversity. While there are still challenges, the spirit of unity and progress shines bright. It's a reminder that even the longest journeys begin with simple steps toward kindness and understanding. Sharing this story with children can help them see the importance of respect, friendship, and community in creating a world where everyone feels valued and included.

Sources: South African Government, Nelson Mandela Foundation, Apartheid Museum, National Geographic, South African Government Official Holidays.

Glossary:

Apartheid: A system of unfair and unequal laws that kept people apart and treated them differently based on their skin color. It was the law in South Africa from 1948 until 1994.

Activist: A person who works to bring about positive changes in the world. Activists use their voice and their actions to make a difference for the people around them.

Equality: Treating everyone the same, no matter their skin color or background.

Fairness: Treating everyone the same way and giving everyone the same chances, no matter who they are.

Rights: Privileges that a government grants to its people. Equal rights mean that all people have the same rights.

Unity: People working together to help each other, acting as one big family even when they are different. Unity is sharing, caring, and playing together happily.

Protest/March: A statement or action expressing disapproval of or objection to something.

Kindness: The quality of being friendly, generous, and considerate.

_____

Sources: South African Human Rights Commission, Human Rights Watch, Cambridge Dictionary, United Nations, South African Government, American Psychological Association, National Geographic, South African Government Official Holidays.

Here's the historical note without numbering, tailored for a children's book:

Important Holidays in South Africa's History

Human Rights Day,

celebrated on March 21, remembers the Sharpeville Massacre in 1960, when people protested against unfair laws. Many were hurt or lost their lives while standing up for their rights. Today, this holiday reminds us that everyone deserves to be treated fairly and with respect.

Freedom Day,

celebrated on April 27, marks the first time all South Africans could vote in 1994. This was a big moment because it ended apartheid, and Nelson Mandela became the first Black president. Freedom Day now reminds us of the importance of equality and democracy.

Youth Day,

on June 16, honors the brave students who protested in Soweto in 1976 against unfair school rules. Many young people were hurt or killed, but their courage helped change South Africa's education system. This holiday celebrates the power of young people to make a difference.

National Women's Day,

on August 9, remembers the 1956 march of thousands of women who protested against unfair laws. It celebrates the strength of women and their role in building a fairer society for everyone.

Reconciliation Day,

celebrated on December 16, is about bringing people together. It's a time for South Africans to remember the past, forgive, and work toward a brighter future. This holiday helps us understand the importance of unity and healing.

Sources: South African Human Rights Commission, Human Rights Watch, Cambridge Dictionary, United Nations, South African Government, American Psychological Association, National Geographic, South African Government Official Holidays.

Activists and Leaders:

Nelson Mandela:

- Leader of the African National Congress (ANC).
- Imprisoned for 27 years for opposing apartheid.
- South Africa's first black president in 1994 promoted peace and reconciliation.
- Won the Nobel Peace Prize in 1993.

Talking Points for Children:

- Explain how Mandela stood up for equal rights for all people in South Africa.
- Highlight his perseverance and kindness despite many years in prison.
- Discuss how he helped bring people together.

Archbishop Desmond Tutu:

- Advocate for equality.
- Awarded the Nobel Peace Prize in 1984 for his efforts.
- Led the Truth and Reconciliation Commission to heal South Africa.

Talking Points for Children:

❯ Describe how Tutu used his voice and his faith to speak out against injustice.

❯ Explain the importance of his work in helping people forgive and move forward after apartheid.

❯ Emphasize his message of love and fairness for everyone.

Albertina Sisulu:

❯ Prominent leader in the ANC Women's League.

❯ Fought for women's rights and was part of many significant protests and movements.

❯ Helped organize the historic 1956 Women's March against apartheid laws.

Talking Points for Children:

❯ Share how Sisulu was a brave woman who stood up for what was right.

❯ Talk about her role in encouraging other women to join the fight for freedom.

❯ Highlight her dedication to helping others through her work as a nurse.

Steve Biko:

❯ Founder of the Black Consciousness Movement.

❯ Advocated for black pride and self-reliance.

❯ Played a key role in inspiring young people to stand up against apartheid.

Talking Points for Children:

❯ Explain how Biko encouraged people to be proud of who they are.

❯ Discuss his belief that everyone deserves to be treated equally.

Winnie Madikizela-Mandela:

❯ Worked tirelessly to continue the fight for freedom while Nelson Mandela was in prison.

❯ Played a significant role in mobilizing communities and raising awareness anti-apartheid campaign.

Talking Points for Children:

❯ Describe how Winnie Madikizela-Mandela was a strong and determined leader.

❯ Talk about her efforts to keep the spirit of the anti-apartheid movement alive.

❯ Highlight her courage and dedication to justice.

Oliver Tambo:

❯ Led the ANC's international campaign against apartheid.

❯ Secured global support and sanctions against the apartheid government.

❯ Played a crucial role in keeping the ANC united and focused during challenging times.

Talking Points for Children:

❯ Share how Oliver Tambo worked from outside South Africa to end apartheid.

❯ Explain his efforts to gather support from other countries.

❯ Emphasize his leadership and commitment to freedom.

These individuals are celebrated for their leadership and activism, both of which were essential in the fight against apartheid and the establishment of a democratic South Africa. This is not meant to be an exhaustive list of anti-apartheid leaders and activists.

Sources: Nelson Mandela Foundation, The Desmond & Leah Tutu Legacy Foundation, South African History Online, National Geographic, South African Government.

www.ingramcontent.com/pod-product-compliance
Lightning Source LLC
Chambersburg PA
CBRC090839120626
46551CB00008B/702

9 7 9 8 2 1 8 3 2 4 1 3 1